GERMAN PERSONNEL CARS IN WARTIME

The light, medium and heavy personnel vehicles of the army

Reinhard Frank

Schiffer Publishing Ltd

1469 Morstein Road, West Chester, Pennsylvania 19380

Inside Front Cover:
Entry of a German news unit into Jakobs-stadt/Dna on June 28, 1941. Steady alternation of a "News Vehicle (M.V. 2) with Mercedes 170 VK chassis" and a "Radio Vehicle (M.V. 23) with uniform chassis II for heavy personnel vehicles". Note the aircraft machine gun on the next-to-last vehicle.

My special thanks to Gertrud, Stefan and Daniel, my friends and helpers Horst Beiersdorf, Johann Demleitner, Siegfried Ehrt, Hermann Freter, Friedrich Masch, Hannes Mayerhofer, N.CSR, Horst Scheibert, Gregor Seidenschwarz, Johann Strauss and Peter Taghon.

SOURCES:
— D600: Durability values of vehicles and devices.
— D662/1-/4: Uniform chassis I for light personnel vehicles.
— D663/1-/3-/11: Uniform chassis for medium personnel vehicles.
— D664/1-/7-/303: Uniform chassis II for heavy personnel vehicles.
— D665/3-/11: Truck 1.5 ton Steyr 1500A/01 & 02.
— Material from firms and archives

Library of Congress Catalog Number: 88-64004.

Translated from German by Dr. Edward Force.
Printed in the United States of America.
ISBN: 0-88740-162-7
Published by Schiffer Publishing, Ltd.
1469 Morstein Road, West Chester, Pennsylvania 19380

This book may be purchased from the publisher.
Please include $2.00 postage.
Try your bookstore first.

FOREWORD

The First World War clearly showed the steadily growing importance of the motor vehicle in warfare. This was also recognized clearly by the German army. When the political pressure on Germany was relaxed and the Allied Military Commissions were withdrawn toward the end of the Twenties, the German army—even though in disguise at first—could carry on a quick motorization of its 100,000 men.

To create the necessary personnel vehicles with cross-country capability, it was necessary to draw on commercially available chassis. They were adapted for cross-country use via increased ground clearance, strengthened springs, locking differentials and the like. The bodywork was completely open; a folding top and rolled side curtains were the only protection from the weather. To keep the occupants from falling out of the car, seats were built with protective sides matching the human body. One sat in them rather as if in a bucket, thus they were called "bucket-seat cars" and "bucket cars" for short. This expression has remained for all further cross-country personnel vehicles, even if they no longer had bucket seats.

The first bucket cars of the German army ran on chassis of the Adler "Favorit" and Mercedes-Benz "Stuttgart" (1927/28).

At the beginning of the Thirties, the idea of a so-called uniform chassis came forth, and was strongly promoted after 1933. One uniform chassis each came into being for the light, medium and heavy personnel vehicles. Parallel to these uniform personnel vehicles, the industry produced their "commercially available" cross-country cars and chassis, which went to the army as so-called "complementary vehicles"—and at the beginning of the war, they formed almost two-thirds of all the army's vehicles.

The following basic types of vehicles can be differentiated:

1. Personnel vehicle (o), commercially available vehicles: civilian vehicles taken over without changes to chassis or body. Theoretically, these cars were to be used only on roads.
2. Personnel vehicle (o) (motor vehicle . . . —commercially available, at best cross-country-capable vehicles developed from civilian chassis with military bodies.
3. Similar to personnel vehicle (o) (motor vehicle . . .)—as before, but with cross-country-capable chassis.
4. Personnel vehicle (E)—cross-country uniform personnel vehicles developed purely for military use.

The individual types of vehicles were given corresponding motor vehicle numbers which classified their type of use but had no connection to manufacturer or type. A group of three Motor Vehicle 15 could consist of one Horch 830 (4 x 2), one Wanderer W11 (4 x 2), each equipped as a news vehicle with medium personnel vehicle (o) chassis and a radio vehicle with uniform chassis (4 x 4) for medium vehicles. All uniform personnel vehicles had all-wheel drive and independent suspension. Some of the light and heavy uniform vehicles had all-wheel steering. The uniform chassis were made by various manufacturers to uniform specifications established by the Army Weapons Office in order to accomplish a standardization of spare parts. Motors from various factories, to some extent interchangeable with each other, were used in uniform construction.

Unfortunately the uniform personnel vehicles did not produce what was expected of them. The vehicles were too complicated and expensive, needed too much service, were hard to repair and much too heavy. In wartime use faults such as breakage of frames, springs and axles, damage to transmissions, steering and clutches appeared: faults that caused long times out of service or, in time of need, total uselessness.

All of this led to the production of uniform vehicles being reduced after 1940 and finally halted altogether.

Even before the war, Major General von Schell had cited in his "Schell Plan" the need for a radical limiting of types for the purpose of achieving commercial mass production. But the German auto industry, which consisted of numerous independent firms, simply could not achieve standardization in the few peacetime years, as the American giants had been able to do. Despite all these difficulties, though, the German army was the continent's best-motorized army at the beginning of the war—both qualitatively and quantitatively.

After the demise of the uniform personnel vehicles, models to put into production had to be found constantly. These included the Mercedes 170 VK and the VW Type 82 to replace the light and medium uniform personnel vehicles and the Steyr 1500 to replace the heavy uniform personnel vehicles.

The total production of German personnel vehicles during the wartime amounted to approximately 200,000 units. Of them some 13,000 units were light, some 15,000 units were medium, and some 5000 units were heavy uniform vehicles, with approximately 20,000 Mercedes 170 VK, 18,000 Steyr 1500 and 52,000 VW 82 units. In the same period almost 640,000 American Jeep units were produced . . .

THE LIGHT PERSONNEL VEHICLES

The civilian types used by the army were cars of up to 1.5 liters in displacement, such as the Opel Olympia, Ford Eifel and the like. The most important bucket cars in this class were the Skoda Popular 1100, Tatra 1.3 type 57 K, VW bucket car, VW amphibian and the light uniform vehicles. Thorough descriptions of the VW types have already appeared in Weapon Arsenal Volumes 58 and 105.

In what follows, the light uniform personnel vehicles will be examined closely.

In D661/1 of April 22, 1940 it is stated: "The uniform chassis I for light personnel motor vehicles is an all-wheel-drive vehicle of a construction type exclusive to the army. The construction of the chassis is uniform to all manufacturers excluding the choice of various motors, lubrication systems and electrical equipment." The first version, which was built from 1936 to 1940, had four-wheel steering. This did not prove useful, since it led to dangerous handling characteristics at speeds over 25 kph and gave no clear advantages in cross-country use. Four different motors were used, all having standardized attachment points and crankshaft couplings: 1. Hanomag 2-liter type 20 B (4 cylinders, 1991 cc, 48 HP at steady speed); 2. BMW 2-liter type 325 (6 cylinders, 1957 cc, 45 HP); 3. Stoewer 1.8-liter type R180W (4 cylinders, 1757 cc, 48 HP); 4. Stoewer 2-liter type AW 2 (4 cylinders, 1997 cc, 48 HP).

The interchanging of motors involved considerable difficulties. The Stoewer 1.8-liter, for example, had the intake manifold on the right and the exhaust manifold on the left—the Stoewer 2-liter had exactly the opposite. There were two different control panels (dashboards), depending on whether or not the uniform switch box was used. The first series was lubricated by hand, whereby 42 lubrication points on the steering and drive train were to be greased with fat every 100 kilometers. For cars with central lubrication, one need only "step once and strongly on the pump pedal" every 50 to 100 kilometers to push motor oil through a system of pipes to the lubrication points.

This lack of uniformity in the uniform vehicles were to be eliminated in 1940 by the "uniform chassis I for light personnel vehicles, type 40". The type 40 had a Stoewer AW 2 two-liter motor, two-wheel steering, oleo-hydraulic instead of cable brakes, uniform switch box, central lubrication and a chassis weight reduced by 100 kg to 1280 kg. The manufacture of chassis and body was now completely entrusted to the Stoewer firm of Stettin. The previously used chassis had been made, other than by Stoewer, by BMW in Eisenach and Hanomag in Hannover; most of the bodies were made by Ambi-Budd in Berlin.

In use, especially under "Russian" conditions, serious damage to frames, suspension, clutch, shafts, steering and the like occurred. But despite all these faults, many former soldiers—with much hindsight—still fondly recall this extraordinarily cross-country-capable and handy vehicle.

The uniform chassis I for light personnel vehicles according to D662/1 of April 22, 1940: 1. Radiator filler cap, 2. Motor, here Hanomag 2-liter type 20 B, 3. Steering, 4. Gearbox with divider drive, 5. battery, 6. Steering switch, 7. Wheel, 8. Main fuel tank and filler cap, 9. Clutch pedal, 10. Brake pedal, 11. Exhaust pipe, 12. Hub, 13. Differential.

Technical Data

UNIFORM CHASSIS I FOR LIGHT PERSONNEL VEHICLE TYPE 40 (ACCORDING TO D662/4)

Motor	
Type:	Stoewer AW 2
Function:	Four-stroke
Stroke:	88 mm
Bore:	85 mm
Cylinders:	4
Displacement (total):	1997 cc
Compression ratio:	1 : 5.8
Sustained performance:	48 hp at 3000 rpm
Top performance:	50 hp at 3500 rpm
Cooling:	Water-cooled by pump
Carburetor:	Solex type 35 BLVF
Lubrication:	Pressure circulation
Chassis	
Clutch:	Single-disc dry
Gears:	5-speed uniform gearbox
Ratio of first gear:	9.12
second gear:	5.01
third gear:	2.86
fourth gear:	1.69
fifth gear:	1
reverse:	7.85
Intermediate gears:	Differential with equalizer gears
Gear ratio:	1.358
Axle drive, front & rear:	Driveshaft and plate wheel
Equalizing gears, front & rear:	Self-locking worm gear by Rheinmetall
Ratio of axle drive:	4.83 (29 : 6)
Drive axles:	2 swing axles
Springs:	Coil springs front & rear
Shock absorbers:	1 double-acting oleo-hydraulic unit per wheel
Foot brake:	Oleo-hydraulic on all four wheels
Hand brake:	Cable on rear wheels
Wheel type & size:	Disc 5"-18
Tires:	600-18 standard country
Steering:	Two-wheel steering
Wheelbase:	2400 mm
Track, front & rear:	1400 mm
Vehicle	
Length:	Depends on body
Height:	Depends on body
Width:	1690 mm
Turning circle diameter:	12.7 meters
Ground clearance:	240 mm
Bottom clearance:	210 mm
Chassis net weight:	1280 kg
Lowest sustained speed:	4 kph
Cruising speed:	70 kph
Top speed in first gear:	9 kph
second gear:	16 kph
third gear:	28 kph
fourth gear:	48 kph
fifth gear:	80 kph
reverse:	10 kph
Climbing ability on a firm surface:	
first gear:	60%
second gear:	42%
third gear:	23%
fourth gear:	13%
fifth gear:	6%
Fording ability:	700 mm
Fuel consumption by norm:	17 liters
Range:	350 km
Fuel capacity, main tank:	50 liters
Fuel capacity, reserve tank:	10 liters

Above: The Dashboard: 1. Oil pressure gauge, 2. Water temperature gauge, 3. Control panel light, 4. High-beam light, 5. Speedometer, 6. Starter button, 7. Throttle, 8. Directional signal, 9. Windshield wiper plug, 10. Uniform switch box, 11. Hand light plug, 12. Radiator shield activator, 13. Clock, 14. Fuel gauge, 15. Securing bar, 16. Central lubrication control.

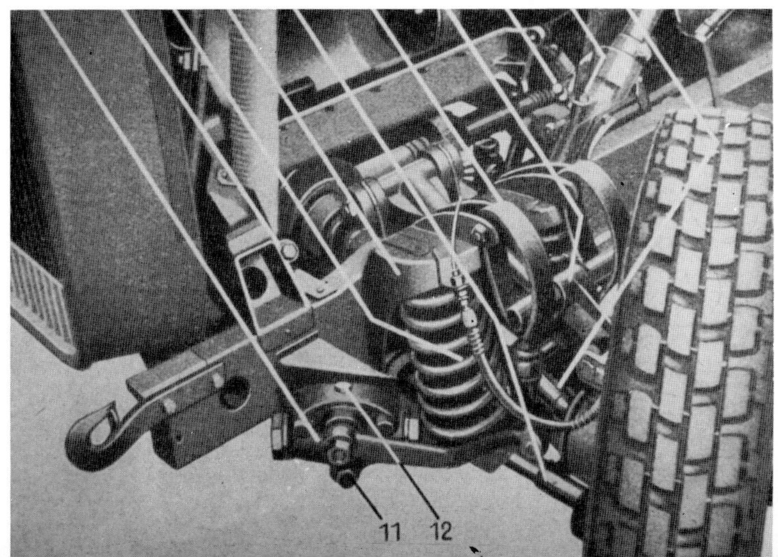

Right:
Front axle of the light uniform personnel vehicle.

Upper left: Light survey troop vehicle (Motor Vehicle 3) with Uniform Chassis I for light vehicles, externally identical to the light cross-country vehicle (M. V. 1). The rear was vertical, the spare wheel on the outside. The radiator grille bars of the 1st uniform personnel vehicle were vertical and, as here, also horizontal. The M. V. 3 had a crew of 4 men, was 3.85 meters long, 1.69 meter wide, 1.90 meter high and had a fighting weight of 2.2 tons.

Above: engine compartment of a 1st uniform personnel vehicle with BMW 2-liter type 325 motor. The numbers refer to the oil tubing for engine lubrication. The oil can at right is significant for the servicing needs of these vehicles.

Left: Small maintenance vehicle (M. V. 2/40). This vehicle had three doors, as did all Motor Vehicle 2, and had a sloping rear; the spare wheel was housed under the sliding workbench. The crew consisted of three men; the external dimensions were the same as Motor Vehicles 1 and 3.

A light uniform personnel vehicle, presumably a "light cross-country-capable personnel vehicle (M. V. 1)", tows a BMW R-75 motorcycle with sidecar. An exact determination of whether this is a "type 40" or an older type of 1st uniform personnel vehicle is not possible on the basis of this photo; only the motor pool sergeant could tell by its papers.

Upper left: On this light uniform personnel vehicle one can clearly see the vertical louvers to let cooling air in and out.

Above: Many of the last uniform personnel vehicles were in use to the end. Here is a burned-out three-door model after the heavy fighting around the Seelow Heights in 1945. Easy to recognize are the double springs on the front and rear axles.

Left: "Through dust and heat toward the Düna, summer 1941". A light universal personnel vehicle of the First Armored Division passes a medium uniform personnel vehicle with the tactical emblem: "Staff company of an armored division" on its staff. Behind it is a 1st uniform personnel vehicle, probably an anti-aircraft car (M. V. 4) with covered double machine guns.

Left:
News vehicle (M. V. 2) with uniform chassis 1 for light personnel vehicles. A three-door vehicle for a three-man crew, with the spare wheel housed on the sloping floor of the trunk.

Right:
A news vehicle (M. V. 2) of the 47th Fla-Battalion in Albania, spring 1941, with bullet holes. The FLA was the anti-aircraft troop of the army, while the FLAK was part of the air force.

Above:
North Africa, 1941, a row of Stukas takes off over a 1st uniform personnel vehicle and an M. V. 2.

Right:
Radio vehicle (M. V. 2) with b1 portable radio transmitter and erected staff antenna. When the top was up, the antenna could be mounted in the antenna socket visible at the rear as a raised vehicle staff antenna.

Above:
Detailed view of the radio vehicle (M. V. 2) with portable radio transmitter d2 and vehicle antenna.

Upper right:
The troop anti-aircraft vehicle (M. V. 4) with uniform chassis I for 1st personnel vehicles had, as did Motor Vehicles 1 and 3, a straight rear with outboard spare wheel, three-man crew and three doors. The armament consisted of two MG 34 guns in a type 36 twin mantlet.

Right:
Troop anti-aircraft vehicle (M. V. 4) of an unidentified SS unit in Budapest. On the spare wheel the type 34 mantlets can be lashed in position around the MG 34 outside the vehicle.

Left:
Imitation battle tank with chassis of the 1st personnel vehicle (o). These training vehicles with the chassis of the commercially available Opel P4 had two-men crews and an MG 34 in the swiveling imitation turret.

Right:
With I.R. 51 (Liegnitz) on "Wehrmacht Day" 1941 this imitation battle tank with chassis of the 1st personnel vehicle (o), WH-5183, was decorated with confident slogans directed at England. Nobody thought about a coming war against Russia. The uniforms of the false Tommies came from the rich booty at Dunkirk. On the left fender is the tactical symbol of the antitank troop. The medium uniform personnel vehicle in the background carries the symbol of the 18th (motorized) I.R. on its fender and driver's door.

Above:
Side view of the "English" 1st uniform personnel vehicle; next to it is a Wanderer W 14.

Above:
In I.R. 54 in Glogau in the spring of 1941 this imitation armored vehicle with uniform chassis 1 for light personnel vehicles was used for training purposes. The wooden body was removable. The emblems are of the 18th (motorized) I.D. and (motorized) Infantry Company.

Right:
On the road from Trondheim to Kirkenes (1940) this "Elf-King" of the 2nd Mountain Division was photographed. Tactical symbol of the 2nd (Infantry) Battalion and Mountain Riflemen (general). It is significant that the rare Mountain Rifle version of the 1st uniform personnel vehicle, with track width decreased to 1250 mm, is shown here, as no previous photos were available.

Upper left:
There has already been much published about the light cross-country personnel vehicle type K 1 (4 x 2) (Volkswagen Type 82), Motor Vehicle 1, the legendary VW "Bucket". Thus it is not necessary to go into greater detail about this vehicle here. The picture shows a well-cared-for VW "Bucket" with the tactical emblem of a general command.

Above:
Changing a wheel of a VW "Bucket". Surely no problem on a paved road, as here—though the air-force man looks quite sour.

Left:
Minor service operations on a VW "Bucket" of the 1st G.D. in Montenegro, 1943.

Upper left:
The VW amphibian was one of the German army's favorite vehicles. Over 14,000 units of this handy cross-country-capable vehicle were built. Here is a light cross-country Type K2 s (4 x 4) (Volkswagen type 166) amphibian, Motor Vehicle 1/20, in Montenegro, 1943. The eagle emblem is unidentified.

Above:
September 1944, Pz. AA 6 in corps reserve. Lieut. Weyersberg and First Sergeant Bussmann with a VW amphibian on a lake east of Gumbinnen. A rare picture, since it shows the type 128, built only in small numbers.

Left:
The same vehicle as above, surrounded by natives.

Left:
The 2nd Mountain Division originated from the 6th Division of the Austrian army (Innsbruck). For this reason the unit used several Steyr Type 250 (4 x 2) 1st personnel vehicles, a reliable 5-seater with water-cooled 4-cylinder boxer motor (25 HP, 1158 cc displacement), of which 1200 units were built. Although a 1st personnel vehicle in terms of size, it was used mainly as a medium personnel vehicle. "With our leader's car at breakfast in Oesterdal (Norway) on September 30, 1942."

Lower left:
A Steyr Type 250 first personnel vehicle of Propaganda Company 621 (Northern Russia, 1942, 18th Army zone).

Below:
In April of 1945 Guben/Neisse could be retaken for a short time. Since suitable vehicles were lacking, confiscated motor-trade vehicles had to fill the holes when needed. Here a Steyr 55 (from which the Type 250 was developed) in original two-tone paint follows a "Hetzer".

THE MEDIUM PERSONNEL VEHICLES

To this group belong all civilian cars with a displacement of from 1.5 to 3.0 liters, such as the BMW 326, Opel Kapitän, Wanderer W 23, Ford V8, Mercedes 170 and the like. Commercially available vehicles with military bodies include in particular the Adler 3 Gd, Horch 830, Wanderer W 11 and W 23 S, Steyr 250 and Mercedes "bucket car" Type 170 VK, 200, 260 and 290.

The Mercedes 170 VK was treated in Arsenal Volume 94. Here we shall have a closer look at the exclusively military construction types, the medium personnel vehicles with "uniform chassis for medium personnel vehicle (with support axle)/(type 40)/(with convertible body)". All these vehicles had 4-wheel drive and 2-wheel steering.

The manufacture of the chassis was done by the Auto Union and Adam Opel firms.

The following chassis numbers are stated in D633 ff:

No. 10,001 ff: Auto Union, Wanderer factory, Siegmar, "support axle", Horch, 3.5 liter V8 motor, 80 HP.

No. 20,001 ff: Auto-Union, Horch factory, Zwickau, otherwise as above.

No. 30,001 ff: Opel, Rüsselsheim/Brandenburg, "support axle", Opel 3.6 liter 6-cylinder in-line motor, 68 HP.

No. 40,001 ff: Auto Union, Wanderer factory, Siegmar, "type 40", Horch 3.5 liter V8 motor, 80 HP.

No. 50,001 ff: a) "Type 40", Horch factory, otherwise as above. b) "convertible body", Horch factory, Horch 3.8 liter V8 motor, 90 HP.

Three bucket cars—three different designs: a 1st uniform personnel vehicle as Motor Vehicle 2 (radio vehicle), two medium uniform personnel vehicles and a VW "Bucket". Cars were often out of action because of the difficulty of getting spare parts, an unavoidable situation, especially under African conditions.

The uniform chassis type 40 differed externally only by the omission of the side support wheels and the lengthened fuel fillers.

Exchanging a Horch motor with an Opel required not only the adapting of fuel and electric lines, motor protection panels, radiator braces and the like, but also a change of clutch including shaft, a partly new exhaust system, new longitudinal drive-shaft, variable/supplementary gears and, depending on the type, a new switching gear.

The medium uniform chassis personnel vehicle also showed serious faults under hard use, in the frame, suspension and power transmission. The D663/1 edition of January 16, 1942 therefore included a section on the strengthening of axles and building in of additional springs in the field.

The chassis with support axles were only partially fitted with central lubrication, while all type 40's had it. The cross-country capability was very limited by the low ground clearance and high fighting weight (for Motor Vehicle 15, approximately 3.3 tons). Even today the motors used in them are much praised for their reliability and power, even if they caused many service problems.

Medium personnel vehicle with uniform chassis for medium personnel vehicles (with support axle), of the air force. The box behind the fender carried tire chains. Notice the air vent on the engine hood. According to HDv. 68/5 of April 1, 1943, there was a medium personnel vehicle (M. V. 12) and one with equipment boxes (M. V. 15). A difference is not recognizable, and the troops spoke almost exclusively of Motor Vehicle 15.

UNIFORM CHASSIS FOR MEDIUM PERSONNEL VEHICLE "TYPE 40" (ACCORDING TO D663/3)

Motor

Model:	Horch
Function:	Four-stroke
Stroke:	92 mm
Bore:	78-mm diameter
Cylinders:	8
Arrangement:	66-degree V
Displacement:	3492 cc
Compression ratio:	6.3 : 1
Steady and top performance (at 3600 rpm):	80 hp
Type of cooling:	Pump-circulated water

Chassis

Clutch:	Single-plate dry Fitchel& Sachs Komet PF 20 KZX
Change gears:	ZF Kb 30 D or Prometheus AGN 18
Number of gears (both types):	4 forward, 1 reverse
Supplementary gears:	Horch
Number of gears:	1 cross-country, 1 normal

Gear ratios for:	Kb 30 D	AGN 18
Reverse:	6.75	5.1
First gear:	5.49	5.47
Second gear:	3.12	2.81
Third gear:	1.80	1.56
Fourth gear:	1	1

Speeds in gears (at 3600 rpm with normal supplementary gears, Klingelnberg gearing):

	Kb 30 D	AGN 18
Reverse:	14 kph	19 kph
First gear:	18 kph	18 kph
Second gear:	31 kph	34 kph
Third gear:	53 kph	62 kph
Fourth gear:	95 kph	95 kph

Supplementary gear ratios:	
Normal gear:	1.097
Cross-country gear:	1.69

Speeds in gears (at 3600 rpm in cross-country gear, Klingelnberg gearing):

	Kb 30 D	AGN 18
Reverse:	9 kph	12 kph
First gear:	11 kph	11 kph
Second gear:	20 kph	22 kph
Third gear:	35 kph	40 kph
Fourth gear:	62 kph	62 kph

Front axle:	Independent suspension, double transverse links (trapeze)
Front wheel drive:	Bevel wheel-plate wheel with spiral gearing
Equalization:	Bevel wheel suspension
Rear axle:	Independent suspension, double transverse links (trapeze)
Rear wheel drive:	Bevel wheel-plate wheel with spiral gearing
Ratio with Klingelnberg gearing:	5.285 = 37 : 7 teeth
Ratio with Gleason gearing:	5.375 = 43 : 8 teeth
Equalization:	Self-locking ZF limited-slip or Rheinmetall wormwheel
Front & rear springs:	2 coil springs per wheel
Shock absorbers per wheel:	2
Construction:	Single- or double-action oleo-hydraulic

Brakes

Foot brake:	Oleo-hydraulic drum brakes on 4 wheels
Hand brake:	Cable drum brakes on both rear wheels
Wheel size:	6"-18
Tires:	190-18 country
Steering type:	ZF-Ross (worm gear) or Münz (inside screw)
Wheelbase:	3100 mm
Track, front & rear:	1532 mm

Vehicle

Overall length:	Depends on body
Chassis length:	4695 mm
Overall width:	1840 mm
Overall height:	Depends on body
Turning circle:	14-meter diameter
Ground clearance:	Approx. 250 mm
Bottom clearance:	Approx. 160 mm
Gross weight (M. V. 12):	3300 kg
Lowest sustained speed:	4 kph
Top speed:	95 kph
Greatest climbing capability in country gear at 3300-kg gross weight:	Approx. 63%
Fording capability:	550 mm
Fuel consumption by norm:	24.5 liters
Oil consumption per 100 km:	Approx. 0.2 liter
Range:	Approx. 400 km
Trailer hitch:	Limber-hook coupling
Height from road to middle of bolt:	Approx. 600 mm
Hitching bolt:	57-mm diameter

Capacities

Water:	Radiator + motor = total: 10 + 10.5 = 20.5 liters
Motor oil in engine-crankcase:	6.5 liters
Oil-bath air filter:	Approx. 0.2 liters
Oil reservoir for central lubrication:	Approx. 1 liter
Change-gear oil for Kb 30 D:	1.5 liters
Change-gear oil for AGN 18:	3 liters
Supplementary gears:	2 liters
Front wheel drive:	1.25 liters
Rear wheel drive:	1.25 liters
Steering gears:	ZB Ross: 0.75 liter
Steering gears:	Münz: 0.78 liter
Brake oil reservoir:	0.5 liter
Fuel (main tank):	70 liters
Fuel (reserve tank):	40 liters

Uniform chassis for medium personnel vehicle with support axle, here as made by Horch.

Upper left:
Medium personnel vehicle (Motor Vehicle 12) with uniform chassis for medium personnel vehicles (according to D600), 4-man crew.

Above:
Medium survey unit vehicle (M. V. 16) or reconnaissance vehicle (M. V. 16/1).

Left:
Interior of a medium uniform personnel vehicle, a convoy leader's car of S.R. 394.

Above:
Medium uniform personnel vehicle with support axle of Engineer Battalion 20 in France, 1940.

Upper right:
The source of our cover picture. A medium uniform personnel vehicle of the 2nd/Engineer Battalion 20 drives around a Czech road barricade during the Sudetenland occupation in 1938. On the rear a small rubber raft, on the sides of the hood the paddles, behind the driver a roll of barrier wire.

Right:
The same vehicle as above with covers on the headlights.

Upper left: Medium uniform personnel vehicle of the detachment doctor of Armored Fusilier Detachment 18 on the return trip after the French campaign.

Above: Standing in a medium uniform personnel vehicle, Colonel Recknagel observes as his I.R. 54 marches by. Also present is a captured, weaponless Renault FT-18 with two Panzer soldiers crammed into its one-man turret.

Left: The medium uniform personnel vehicle of an army Fla unit in Greece. Notice the louvers instead of flaps in the engine hood. Behind it is a Steyr 640 ambulance.

Above:
Rear-guard action of I.R. 61 on September 5, 1943 at Novgorod Szeverski. The medium uniform personnel vehicle carries the standard of the division commander. On the fender is the emblem of the 7th I.D. and the staff pennant.

Upper right:
Rear view of a medium uniform personnel vehicle of the Motorcycle Battalion 402 at Tudulina in the summer of 1941, passing a Russian 1939-model T-26 S.

Right: this medium uniform personnel vehicle of the first G.D. drove onto a mine on May 21, 1942.

Left: Airmen applying winter paint (chalk?) to a medium uniform personnel vehicle with support axle.

Lower left: Servicing a medium uniform personnel vehicle in April of 1941 "at the foot of Olympus". The vehicle belonged to either Fla Battalion 1/47, 2/47 or 3/609. The motor can be identified definitely as a Horch.

Below: Southern sector of the Eastern Front, 1941, 1st G.D. General Lutz, wearing the Knight's Cross, and OTL Lang in a medium uniform personnel vehicle. Since the vehicle shows an antenna console, it may be a radio vehicle (M. V. 15). The hunting rifles in the rifle racks are purely private in nature.

Upper left:
Radio vehicle (Motor Vehicle 15) with bl or f portable radio transmitter.

Above:
A radio vehicle (M. V. 17) with uniform chassis for medium personnel vehicles (with support axle) of the 6th P.D. returning over the Dnieper in the fall of 1943. To carry the chicken supply, the frame antenna was covered with wire mesh and turned into a henhouse. On the fender is a sack of chicken feed. The mast antenna at the rear remains for the radio.

Left:
The size of the uniform chassis for medium personnel vehicles allowed a number of box bodies for a variety of uses, all called Motor Vehicle 17. The picture shows a cable-measuring vehicle: 3-man crew, fighting weight 3.5 tons, length 4.80 meters, width 1.80 meters, height 1.85 meters.

Right:
Uniform chassis for medium personnel vehicles, type 40: 1. Attachment for headlight masking, 2. Headlights, 3. Radiator filler cap, 4. Flagstaff, 5. Oil reservoir for central lubrication, 6. Horn button, 7. Dashboard, 8. Gearshift lever, 9. Supplementary gear lever, 10. Battery (12-volt), 11. Main fuel tank filler, 12. Rear wheel drive, 13. Reserve fuel tank filler, 14. Tow hook, 15. Electric connection for trailer, 16. Muffler, 17. Chain box, 18. Flagstaff, 19. Cross member.

Left:
Photos of Motor Vehicle 17 with the uniform chassis for medium personnel vehicles, type 40, thus without support axles, are rare. Here is a radio vehicle of the "Grossdeutschland" Armored Grenadier Division.

Right:
The 18th I.D. was changed to a motorized division only in 1940/41. That is why it received mainly the medium uniform personnel vehicles of Type 40. Here is the car of OTL Schmeling, Commander of Engineer Battalion 18; standing is Lt. Melzer, the Battalion Adjutant. In the foreground is a Horch 830 R. The location is Daschki, northeast of Vilna, circa June 30, 1941.

Left:
OTL Schmeling reports to Major General Herrlein, the Commander of the 18th (motorized) I.R.. On the left fender of this medium uniform personnel vehicle, type 40, is the "Division Command" symbol. The side-curtains are attached to keep out dust.

Above: Vehicles of the "Grossdeutschland" Armored Grenadier Division in the Tomarovka area, spring 1943. In front is a radio vehicle (M. V. 15) with uniform chassis for medium personnel vehicles, Type 40. Tactical emblem: Staff of Artillery Regiment (motorized). Behind it is a radio vehicle (M. V. 2) with the uniform chassis I for light personnel vehicles, followed by two radio vehicles (M. V. 17/1) with staff antennas and two radio vehicles (M. V. 17) with frame antennas.

Right: A medium uniform personnel vehicle, type 40, of the air force between Berisino and Mius. The sergeant wears the Demjansk emblem, thus the picture must have been taken after April of 1943. (H. Hoppe)

Right:
Medium personnel vehicle with uniform chassis for medium personnel vehicles, type 40, of the 1st P.D., with battalion pennant. One can recognize the inboard spare wheel and the three-seat rear bench, which became possible when the bodywork was widened.

Left:
Rommel in a medium uniform personnel vehicle, type 40. In front of the rear seats is a worktable, as was customary for Motor Vehicle 16 (with survey troop emblem). The two tank filler caps are easy to see.

Upper left: For the highest government officials there was a special version of the medium uniform chassis for medium personnel vehicles: the "uniform chassis for medium personnel vehicles with convertible body, without support axle, with Horch 3.8-liter motor". This is General Landgraf's car in 1941 at the Düna, where an army report is being heard. Recognizable are the division and general's pennants, plus the symbols for division command and 6th P.D. on the fender.

Above: The convertible of Senior General Guderian (left) in Russia, summer 1941, with air recognition marking on the engine hood and General Command/Armored Unit symbol.

Left: Field Marshal List in Greece, 1941, in his convertible with army group command and field marshal emblems. In the background is a medium uniform personnel vehicle with support axle.

Right: The Horch 830 R, of which more than 4000 units were built since 1934, was very widespread in the first years of the war. The chassis corresponded to the commercially available medium personnel vehicle (4 x 2). The Horch V-8 motor produced 70 HP. In the picture are two Horch 830 R as news vehicles (M. V. 15) with I.R. 61 at the Zwardon Pass (September 1, 1939). In front is the subsequent regimental commander, First Lieutenant Nagerl.

Outside right: Horch 830 R of the 4th P.D. with tactical symbol of a motorized cavalry unit, on the Somme.

Below: A Horch 830 R as staff car of an engineer battalion on France.

Upper left: News vehicle (M. V. 15) with chassis of the medium personnel vehicle (o) Horch 830 R.

Above: A Horch 830 R shortly before the war began, in the second convoy of Engineer Battalion 14. At left the convoy leader (later OTL) Friedrich Masch. The vehicle has the cooling flaps of the 1934 model. The motorcycle courier sits on a BMW R 12 (750 cc).

Left: The 14th Company of I.R. 61 with a 3.7-cm antitank gun on a training march. This early version of the Horch 830 R has a shortened body to make room for two removable containers on the back, and was classified as a "medium personnel vehicle with towing apparatus (M. V. 12) on the chassis of the medium personnel vehicle (o)".

Left:
The best-looking of all "bucket cars" was probably the Mercedes-Benz Stuttgart 260. It was built from 1929 to 1935 and had a straight 6-cylinder motor with 2.6-liter displacement and 50-HP performance. The picture shows the Fla Instructional Company (Captain von der Mosel) in the 1936 Leader's Parade in Berlin.

Right:
This Mercedes-Benz Stuttgart 260 was still being used in 1942 by the Geb.Pz.Jg.Abt. 44.

Above:
The Mercedes 170 VK was the second most frequently built "bucket car", after the VW Bucket, and was very popular because of its reliability. These two naval men are spending a peaceful day with their convertible in Le Havre. Note the vertical rear of this model.

Right:
This Mercedes 170 VK has faced much worse conditions; it is a "News Vehicle (M. V. 2) with chassis of the medium personnel vehicle (o)" of the 101st I.D. in the Kharkov area, fall 1941.

Upper left:
Another manufacturer of "bucket cars" was the Adler firm. Here is an Adler Type 12 N-RW (4 x 2), built in 1932/33, of the 14th/I/R/ 74 with an ammunition trailer (Sd.Ah. 32)

Above:
With over 4000 units built, the Adler Type 3 Gd (4 x 2) was quite common. The vehicle shown here belongs to M.G. Battalion 6, as the lettering shows.

Left: The Adler Type 3 Gd of a commanding general. More precise information is unfortunately not available.

Upper left:
More than 5500 units of the Wanderer W 11 (4 x 2) were produced between 1933 and 1941. Here is a company troop car of the 14th I.D. (1935).

Above:
Exhausted soldiers of Motorcycle Battalion 402 during the French campaign. Amid them is the massive snout of a Wanderer W 11.

Left: A Wanderer W 11 before the war. The vehicle had a straight 6-cylinder motor with 2.5 liter displacement and 50 HP performance.

Upper left: Only a few examples of the Stoewer M 12 reached the army. Here is a Motor Vehicle 12 (medium personnel vehicle (o) with towing apparatus) of S.R. 4 in Lithuania.

Above: This is what the rear box of a bucket car (type?) looked like after long use. France 1940, 14th/I.R. 74.

Left: Not very common either was the Wanderer W 23 S. The picture shows a vehicle (WH 754924) of the Guderian Armored Grenadiers, which has been hit.

THE HEAVY PERSONNEL VEHICLES

Among the purely civilian types, these were the cars of over 3.0-liter displacement, such as the Mercedes 320, 540 and 770, Horch 830 and 930, and Opel Admiral. Among the commercially available chassis with military bodies, the Skoda Superb 3000, Steyr 1500, Mercedes L 1500 and Phänomen Granit 1500, among others, fell into this class. There were also vehicles with three-axle truck chassis, such as the Mercedes G 4, Steyr 640 and Krupp L 2 H 143. The corresponding construction for the army alone was the "uniform chassis II for heavy personnel vehicles". We shall have a closer look at this chassis and its successor, the Steyr 1500.

The uniform chassis II for heavy personnel vehicles was built by Auto Union at the Horch factory in Zwickau and the Ford factories in Cologne-Niehl and Berlin. As for the chassis number (FG . . .) in D664 ff, let us look at the tangle of red tape:

- FG. 100 001-100 350: "type a" 4-wheel steering (up to 25 kph), switchable to 2-wheel steering, divided Horch transverse link shafts, mechanical brakes, Horch 3.5 liter V8 motor, 80 HP.
- FG. from 100 351 on: "type 1a", 4-wheel steering, switchable to 2-wheel steering, Rhein-Metall transverse link shafts, oil-pressure brakes, Horch 3.8 liter V8 motor, 81 HP.
- FG. 120 001-120 650: "type b", 2-wheel steering, otherwise as Type a.
- FG. from 120 651 on, "type 1b", 2-wheel steering, otherwise as Type 1a.
- FG. from 140 001 on, "type 1c", 2-wheel steering, only for bodies with armored sides.

In these vehicles the filler caps for the main and reserve fuel tanks were inside. All vehicles had support axles (except type 1c) and were made by Horch.

FG. from 300 001 on: made by Ford:

- "Type EGa", 4-wheel steering (up to 25 kph), switchable to 2-wheel steering, oil-pressure brakes, support axles, Ford V8 3.6-liter motor, 78 HP, fuel fillers extended to the side.
- "Type EGb", as above, but with 2-wheel steering.
- "Type EGd", as type EGa but without support axles.

FG. from 400 001 on: "Type 40", made by Horch, with Horch 3.8 liter V8 motor, 90 HP.

FG. from 500 001 on, "Type 40", made by Ford, with Ford 3.6 liter V8 motor, 78 HP.

All models had a central lubrication system. Depending on their purpose, they had 130, 300 or 600-watt generators built in. In the "type 40" the all-wheel steering and support axles had been eliminated; the fuel fillers were extended to the side.

When in use, these vehicles often had frame and spring breakage. An addition to D664/1/7 appeared: "Axle strengthening and addition of extra springs", to avoid damage. The heavy uniform personnel vehicles were very popular among the troops because of their roominess. They were intended for the same uses as the 3-axle Krupp L 2 H143 light truck (o). Like all uniform personnel vehicles, the heavy type suffered from its complicated body and high weight. The gross weight of a Motor Vehicle 70 with heavy uniform chassis was 3150 kg, with Steyr 1500 A chassis only 2485 kg. The Steyr 1500 A and the Mercedes L 1500 replaced the heavy uniform personnel vehicle from 1941 on. The chassis of the Steyr 1500 A was intended for "1.5 ton trucks". The manufacture of chassis and bodies was done by Steyr-Daimler-Puch in Steyr and under license by Auto-Union at its Siegmar factory. The Steyr 3.5 liter V8 air-cooled motor and 75 HP sustained performance was used. The vehicles had 4-wheel drive, central lubrication and oleo-hydraulic brakes.

There were the Steyr 1500 A/01 and later 1500 A/02 models which, other than in minor details, differed only in the different locations of the spare wheel.

These vehicles proved themselves well with the troops, they were reliable and required little service.

Technical Data

UNIFORM CHASSIS II FOR HEAVY PERSONNEL VEHICLES TYPE 40 (ACCORDING TO D664/7)

	Horch (Auto Union)	Ford
Motor		
Function	Four-stroke	Four-stroke
Stroke	100 mm	95 mm
Bore	78 mm	77.8 mm
Cylinders	8	8
Arrangement	66-degree V	90-degree V
Displacement	3823 cc	3613 cc
Compression	6.1 : 1	6.15 : 1
Performance	90 hp at 3600 rpm	78 hp at 3500 rpm
Lubrication	Pressure pump	Pressure pump
Cooling	Circulating pump	Circulating pump
Carburetor	1 Solex BFLH, 1 Solex BFRH	1 Solex 30 FFIK
Fuel pump	Solex PE 888	Ford-Solex
Clutch	1-plate dry Fitchel & Sachs, Komet PF24KM/H	1-plate Ford with mechanical damping and flywheel
Chassis		
Variable gears	Unified with drive to 2 axles by a divider gear lockable by hand	
Gears	1 country, 4 forward, 1 reverse	
Gear ratios		
Country	10.90	10.90
First gear	6.28	6.28
Second gear	4.20	4.20
Third gear	2.46	2.46
Fourth gear	1.48	1.48
Reverse	10.90	10.90
Wheel drive ratio	4 .37	5.14
Speeds in gears (at 3600 rpm)		
Country	12 kph	10 kph
First gear	21 kph	18 kph
Second gear	32 kph	27 kph
Third gear	54 kph	46 kph
Fourth gear	90 kph	76 kph
Reverse	12 kph	10 kph
Front axle	Independent suspension, double transverse links	

	Horch (Auto Union)	Ford
Lowest sustained speed in gear		
Country	5 kph	2.5 kph
Top speed	90 kph	85 kph
Climbing ability in gear		
Country	46.2%	35.9%
First gear	25.7%	19.4%
Second gear	16.5%	12.0%
Third gear	8.3%	5.7%
Fourth gear	3.9%	2.2%
Reverse	46.2%	35.9%
Fuel consumption	28 liters	35 liters
Range	425 km	345 km
Fording ability	500 mm	750 mm
Capacities		
Cooling water	23 liters	26 liters
Motor oil	8 liters	4.5 liters
Main fuel tank	55 liters	55 liters
Reserve tank	65 liters	65 liters

Details common to both types:

Equalization, front	Bevel wheel
Equalization, rear	Worm gear
Suspension, front & rear	Two coil springs per wheel
Shock absorbers, per wheel	Two
Type	Single- or double-acting oleo-hydraulic
Foot brake	Oleo-hydraulic drum brakes on all four wheels
Hand brake	Cable drum brakes on all four wheels
Wheel size	7"-18
Tires	210-18 country
Steering	Two-wheel
Type	ZF-Ross (worm gear) or Münz (inside screw)
Wheelbase	3000 mm
Track, front & rear	1646 mm
Vehicle	
Chassis length	4760 mm
Chassis width	2000 mm
Turning circle	15 meters
Ground clearance, fully laden	Approx. 260 mm
Bottom clearance, fully laden	Approx. 260 mm
Chassis weight	2300 kg

Left:
Uniform chassis II for heavy personnel vehicles, type 40: 1. Staff, 2. Masked headlight, 3. Radiator cap, 6. Variable gear switching lever, 7. Divider gear switching lever, 8. Chain box (also 14 & 16), 9. Reserve fuel tank, 10. Rear wheel drive, 11. Main fuel tank, 15. Battery.

Right:
Uniform chassis II for heavy personnel vehicles, type a/1a: 2. Main fuel tank, 6. Reserve fuel tank, 11, (also 23 & 28) Tire chain box, 12. Change gears, 22. Two-step main brake cylinder, 27. Steering switching gear.

Above:
Limber vehicle (M. V. 69) with uniform chassis II for heavy personnel vehicles, holding six men. There was also a light version of Motor Vehicle 69, the "Limber vehicle with chassis of the light truck (o)", the Krupp-Protze. The heavy personnel vehicles were planned for the same tasks as the light trucks!

Above:
Personnel car (M. V. 70) with uniform chassis II for heavy personnel vehicles; holding eight men.

Left:
Light searchlight power vehicle II (M. V. 83) with uniform chassis II for heavy personnel vehicles, holding five men.

Above:
Radio vehicle (M. V. 23) with uniform chassis II for heavy personnel vehicles, holding seven men. The horizontal louvers on the sides of the motor hood and the low number of them on the top are noteworthy.

Above:
Light searchlight power vehicle I (M. V. 83) with uniform chassis II for heavy personnel vehicles, holding five men.

Left:
There were also heavy uniform personnel vehicles with box bodies, such as this amplifier vehicle (M. V. 24). The ambulance (M. V. 31) had a very similar body.

Left:
Personnel vehicles (M. V. 70) of the 3rd Kp.S.R. ready to move out of Osterode, East Prussia on June 17, 1941 for night drill—a "drill" that was to last for years.

Right:
This personnel vehicle (M. V. 70) belonged to the 6th P.D. (motorized marksmen) in Iserlohn in 1940. According to the text, it should be a Horch. It is impossible to identify the type of a heavy uniform personnel vehicle without the chassis number.

Volkov Front, 1942! [The sign says: "Don drive in the ruts like a Zeppelin on rails, you dummy!"]

Above:
Map study by the staff of Geb.Pz.Jg.Abt. 44 at the beginning of the Russian campaign. The heavy uniform personnel vehicles of this unit had the headlight masking mounted on the middle of the motor hood.

Right:
Detailed picture of personnel vehicles (M. V. 70) of the Geb.Pz.Jg.Abt. 44 in France, 1940. At left is Johann Demleitner, "the Smith of Kochel".

Left:
Winter camouflage paint for a heavy uniform personnel vehicle in Russia, 1941. The car is given a garage to protect it from the winter, but the senior corporal does not even have gloves, to say nothing of winter clothing.

Right:
A convoy of the 3rd/FLA 601 in the middle sector of the Eastern Front in October of 1941. In front is the convoy leader's car, a heavy uniform personnel vehicle, followed by a 1-ton towing truck with 2 cm anti-aircraft gun. At left is a Russian GAZ-AA.

Upper left:
In the Gives area of Belgium is a destroyed heavy uniform personnel vehicle of the 1st G.D.

Above:
In Karacho this heavy uniform personnel vehicle hurries past Russian tanks (BT 7 1935 model and T 26) toward Schaulon. Here the mounting of the outward-hanging doors on the rear can be seen.

Left:
Ferrying heavy uniform personnel vehicles of Motorcycle Battalion 402 across the Düna south of Riga on July 1, 1941.

Right:
Photos taken during the retreat in the winter of 1941/42 are rare. Here a 2 cm anti-aircraft gun 30 (28 kills!) with the limber vehicle prepared for it, a heavy uniform personnel vehicle (HGr. Center, 216th I.D., I.R. 398).

Below:
2-cm anti-aircraft gun 38 (Sf) on a heavy uniform personnel vehicle, a rebuilt version that came into use in only small numbers.

Left:
In the ravines north of Bielgorod are concealed vehicles of the 6th P.D. (July 1943). At right a heavy uniform personnel vehicle type 40, as well as a uniform diesel (on which a Weapon Arsenal volume is in preparation), a Mercedes 170 VK and a VW bucket car.

Lower left:
Radio vehicle (M. V. 23) with uniform chassis II for heavy personnel vehicles, type 40.

Below:
Abandoned radio vehicle (M. V. 23) of an unknown unit.

Upper left:
The 1.5-ton Steyr truck (4 x 4) was the successor to the heavy uniform personnel vehicle. The picture shows the early production type (Steyr) of the personnel car, model 1500 A/01, with air-cooled Steyr V8 85 HP 3.5 liter engine.

Above:
The 1.5 ton Steyr truck, model 1500 A/02 had its spare wheel mounted outboard. The vehicle held eight men, the motor was the same as that of model 1500 A/01.

Left:
From 1942 to 1944 the Steyr 1.5 ton Steyr truck was made by Steyr and Auto-Union as model 1500 A/02.

Steyr 1.5 ton truck, model 1500 A/01, of Fla Battalion 22, in the southern sector of the Eastern Front. Behind it is a Sd.Kfz. 10/5.

Left:
The 6th P.D. crosses the Don at Potemkinskaya on December 25, 1942, after the relief attack in the direction of Stalingrad. On the bridge ramo is a Steyr 1.5 ton truck, model 1500 A/02.

Below:
A "Fieseler Stork" flies over a Steyr 1500 A/02. Because of its air-cooled motor, the Steyr was very popular in Africa.

Below:
A Steyr 1500 A (probably 01) with type 34 machine guns in a twin mantlet on an African airfield. In the background is a "Weihe".

In closing, three more vehicles that were used as heavy personnel vehicles:

Upper left:
There were only two of the separately armored Krupp L2 H 43 with mounted 3.7 cm antitank guns. The armor was supplied by Skoda to plans by First Lieutenant Kaiser (Geb.Pz.Jg.Abt. 44). On the march the gun crew sat on the rear seats. The picture shows one of these rarities in the Uman area in 1941, in full action.

Above: Taken over from the Austrian army was this Steyr type 640 (6 x 4) with the rare group car body. One sees it here fully occupied by officers of Engineer Battalion 14 in Giurgiu, Rumania.

Left: A Phänomen Granit 1500 as Motor Vehicle 31 at Kuban.